Fun Spider Facts for Kids

Jacquelyn Elnor Johnson

www.CrimsonHillBooks.com

First edition, August 2025.

Cataloguing in Publication Data

Johnson, Jacquelyn Elnor

Fun Spider Facts for Kids

Description: Crimson Hill Books trade paperback edition | Nova Scotia, Canada

ISBN:	978-1-990887-83-3 (Paperback - Ingram)
BISAC:	JNF003120 Juvenile Fiction: Animals – Insects, Spiders, Etc.
	JNF003170 Juvenile Nonfiction: Animals – Pets
	JNF016000 Juvenile Nonfiction: Curiosities & Wonders
THEMA:	PSVA8 - Arachnids (arachnology)
	WNGX - Insects & spiders as pets
	YNNL - Children's - Teenage general interest: Insects, spiders, minibeasts

Record available at https://www.bac-lac.gc.ca/eng/Pages/home.aspx

Book design: Jesse Johnson

Crimson Hill Books
(a division of)
Crimson Hill Products Inc.
Lawrencetown, Nova Scotia
Canada

Crimson Hill
Books

They're small.

They always have 8 legs but no feet.

Some are beautiful.

Others are fierce.

A few can be deadly.

Most Spiders are shy and secretive creatures.

Spiders have secrets!

Spiders are your neighbors and probably also live in your home – but how much do you really know about them?

An ancient animal, some of them almost unchanged for millions of years, Spiders live where we do. They're in the fields, in our backyards and they also live where we do. Yet we rarely see them because they're small and shy. They'd much rather hide or scurry away than have to meet any humans.

Spiders live strange and secret lives. They have odd ways and some even odder abilities, doing things no other animal can do. Even more remarkable is they are born knowing how to do these things. Unlike most other animals, Spider parents don't teach their babies survival skills.

One ability all Spiders have is spinning silk. They use their silk in many ingenious ways. They craft their webs with silk, they parachute and hang-glide with it and they cocoon their eggs with silk.

While Spiders are known for spinning webs, not all of them do. There's also a lot of variety in where they choose to live. Spiders live almost everywhere on earth except the very far North and Antarctica. Those places are too cold for them.

Is it an insect, or a Spider?

All Insects Have:	**All Spiders have:**
A hard exoskeleton outside their bodies	A hard exoskeleton, similar to insects
6 legs	8 legs
Antennae	No antennae
No spinnerets	Spinnerets to make silk
Some have venom	All have venom
No fangs	All have fangs
Many insects can fly	Spiders can't fly
Strong legs	Weak legs
Usually are colorful	Most are brown or black

All Spiders make silk. They can control the silk they make and can create silk for many different purposes.

What is a spider?

Spiders all have eight legs and a hard exoskeleton. They all have two body parts, a head and abdomen. They all have hollow fangs that deliver venom. And almost all of them have lots of eyes, always in pairs on their heads. But even with all their eyes, most Spiders have poor eyesight and some can't see at all.

Spiders are meat-eaters. They have an amazing variety of hunting skills and techniques. Some Spider species are even able to change their hunting strategy, depending on the prey. Often that prey is several times larger than they are.

One reason you might not have noticed Spiders that often is that many of them are nocturnal. This means they sleep all day and are active at night.

Spiders have no internal bones. Their bodies are totally soft inside, the same as insects' bodies are, protected by their hard outer body shell called an exoskeleton. Like insects, Spiders have no spine and no skeleton.

Another way that Spiders are like insects is both have no teeth. They can't chew their food. Spiders can't even eat solid food. Everything they eat has to be a liquid.

Like insects, Spiders need to shed their exoskeleton in order to grow. This is called molting. Spiders need to molt many times to reach adulthood. Most types of Spiders stop molting when they become adults, but there are some species that continue molting for their entire lives.

To molt, first they spin a screen around themselves, something like stepping into their own dressing room. It takes about two hours for a spider to shed its old exoskeleton, have its new one dry hard and be able to step out from behind its silk changing screen.

Spiders have no muscles in their legs. They have to pump blood into their legs to strengthen them when they want to run or jump.

Spiders use color for camouflage to help hide them from their enemies. Their major enemies are parasitic wasps and birds. Both these enemies can see colors, so Spiders have colors that help them disappear into the background of where they live. Some Spiders are more colorful, with stripes, dots or designs on their backs meant to work like camo, confuse their predators or attract their mates.

Some Spiders can walk on glass and can even walk upside down on ceilings. They can do this because they have two claws on the ends of their legs. These claws have fine bristles, called scopulae (say this: skop-you-lay) between their claws. The scopulae have as many as 1,000 tiny branches that can cling on to very thin layers of water on surfaces.

Sea Spiders got their name because they look like land Spiders. They live in all of the world's oceans.

Sea Spiders aren't actually Spiders

Sea Spiders are distant cousins of land Spiders. Though they have the Spider name, Sea Spiders aren't actually Spiders. They're arthropods, just like Spiders, but they belong to a different order of animals with a funny name, Pantopoda [say this: PAN-toe-poe-da].

A healthy meadow has more than 2 million Spiders per acre or almost half a hectare in summer.

This web was made by an orb-weaving Spider.

Spiders spin silk

Spider silk is very light, bendy, and stretchy. It might look wispy, but it's surprisingly strong.

Their silk could be spun as just a single thread, or as many threads together for extra strength. It might be sticky, or not. Spiders know all the types and thicknesses of silk they can spin and the different uses for their different types of silk.

They wrap their eggs in it to protect them. They build silk webs to catch their prey and then wrap the prey once it's caught. They might use their silk to build a shelter to hide in while they molt or to line their underground homes. Some Spiders can hang in the air on a silk safety line.

Spiders make their silk using the spinnerets on their abdomens. They can have 4, 6 or 8 spinnerets depending on what type of Spider they are. Each spinneret has many spigots. A spigot is a tap. These spigots are attached to silk glands inside their abdomens. Inside their bodies, spider silk is a liquid. It doesn't become a thread until it dries as soon as it is outside their bodies.

They don't shoot silk out of their abdomens. Spiders need to pull the silk out with their legs.

There are six types of silk glands and possibly more say some arachnologists (say this: ARR-akk-naw-low-jists). Arachnologists are scientists who study Spiders. Each type of silk gland makes a different type of silk.

A Spider can spin 700 meters or 765 yards of silk in one continuous strand.

Where did Spiders come from?

Though Spiders have been on earth for a very long time, there is still a lot we don't know about how they evolved. What we do know is the first Spider-like animals that lived on land lived about 420 million years ago.

Spiders by numbers:

386 million years ago	the earliest silk-spinning Spiders appeared
318 to 200 million years ago	modern Spiders evolved in China
51,673 species	that we know of today
8	number of legs they have
0, 6, 8 or 12	number of eyes they have
2 years	average number of years a wild spider lives
1 species	is vegetarian. All the rest eat other animals

Spider fossils are very rare. Only about 1,000 have been found, most of them preserved in amber. Amber is a clear orange stone made of the sap of an ancient tree that slowly hardened. The oldest amber Spider fossil ever found has a Spider inside it that lived 130 million years ago. The oldest amber fossil Spider web is dated to 100 million years ago.

The earliest Spiders lived in underground barrows. They lined their burrows with Spider silk and built a hidden trap door at the entrances to their burrows. Trapdoor Spiders still exist. They still look and behave very much like their ancient ancestors. Most modern Spiders live above ground.

What do Spiders eat?

Almost all Spiders are meat-eaters. The only type of Spider that prefers to eat plants is *Bagneera kiplingi*. It is a type of jumping Spider that lives in Mexico, Costa Rica and Guatemala. This Spider lives in acacia trees because the trees have nubs on the ends of the leaves that they like. They have another unusual food craving, for a Spider – plant nectar. They also have a taste for ant larvae.

Some types of Spiders eat nectar when they are young but stop when they're adults. All other Spiders eat ants, flies, mosquitoes, and bees. Larger species also eat small animals like birds, frogs, lizards and centipedes. And most Spiders eat other Spiders.

Spiders can only eat liquid food. They have to liquify their prey before they can eat it. They do this by injecting their venom into a struggling victim. This venom starts to turn the victims' insides into liquid. A Spider wraps their future food in silk that also has venom to break down the victim's body.

Spiders have two pedipalps below their mouths. Pedipalps used to be extra legs, but over millions of years they evolved to be mouth parts, helping Spiders grab and hold onto their food. When they cannot find or trap food, Spiders can live for several months without eating.

Tarantulas can be up to 90 millimeters or 3.5 inches long. The world's largest Tarantulas are 243 times as big as the world's smallest Spiders!

This Spider has captured a baby bat.

How do Spiders get their prey?

Many animals use vibrations to survive, including Spiders.

Spiders are hyper-sensitive to even the tiniest vibrations in their webs. When they feel even the slightest twitch, they rush over to find out what has blundered into their web and is caught there. They quickly wrap the victim in silk, like high-speed shrink wrapping. Then they sting to paralyze the victim with their venom. The venom also turns the victim's insides into a liquid. That's when the hungry Spider sucks it out, leaving the legs, wings, and other parts it can't digest.

How long do Spiders live?

Most wild Spiders don't live very long, usually only about two years, though some can live much longer if they live in a protected place like a wildlife park.

In most Spider species females live longer than males. Males usually die soon after mating for the first time, sometimes because the females eat them to have extra energy for laying their eggs.

Social Spiders

Most Spiders prefer to live alone. There are some species that are very social, living in groups, cooperating to care for their eggs and Spiderlings, hunting together and sharing food. Spiderlings are baby spiders.

The largest Spider colony ever found had 50,000 Spider members.

Widow Spiders live alone and are cannibals, aggressively attacking each other. But when they are captive, like at a zoo or in a scientist's lab, they will form colonies, sharing their webs and their food and not attacking each other. Scientists aren't sure why being captive changes their behavior this much.

Carparachne aureoflava lives in the desert in Namibia, Africa. To escape parasitic wasps, it flips onto its side and cartwheels down sand dunes to make a quick getaway.

Jumping Spiders have very good eyesight. This is unusual, for Spiders.

What can Spiders see?

Most Spiders that have eyes are near-sighted. This means they can only see things that are close with their eight, six, four or two eyes, depending on what type of Spider they are. Spiders can see in blue and green and can also see UV light. They cannot see red, yellow or orange.

Spiders that are active hunters, like Wolf Spiders and Jumping Spiders, are the ones with the sharpest eyesight.

Some species of Spiders have eyes that can't see or no eyes and are blind, but that doesn't stop them from finding their prey and even stealing it from other Spiders' webs. Most of the totally blind Spiders live underground in caves.

What can Spiders hear?

Spiders have no ears. Most Spiders can barely hear anything. Instead, they sense vibrations. That's their superpower.

They use touch sensors on the ends of their legs. These sensors can feel even the slightest breeze or movement on their webs or the ground.

What else can Spiders feel?

Most Spiders have hairs on their legs that detect the flow of either water or air. Their bodies are covered with thousands of slit sensillae. These are vibration cracks around their joints that can sense vibrations from whatever they're standing on.

Spiders can also sense electric fields around animals and other living things like plants and trees.

Some speed demon Spiders can run 2 miles or 3.2 kilometers per hour. That might sound slow to you, but when you compare by body sizes, it's like a man being able to run 140 miles or 225 kilometers per hour, something no human can do.

Spiders don't have noses, but they all have a strong sense of smell.

What can Spiders smell?

Spiders are very good at using smell-o-vision. This means they can identify other creatures, like prey, enemies, or a possible mate just by their smells. Arachnologists, the spider experts, call this using chemical sensors.

Chemical sensors are like a combination of taste and smell, but not by using a nose or taste buds in their mouths, because Spiders don't have these. Instead, they do their chemical sensing with hairs on their legs or bristles on their pedipalps. Male Spiders have more chemical-sensing pedipalp bristles than females. This helps them find females to mate with.

Smells that Spiders hate

These are the odors that will send Spiders rushing away:

- Any citrus fruit like lemons, oranges or limes
- Peppermint oil
- Tea tree oil
- Eucalyptus oil
- Vinegar

There are 51,673 species of Spider that we know of and probably more we haven't yet discovered. Of all of them, only one is vegetarian. That's Bagheera kiplingi, a type of Jumping Spider that lives in Central America.

This Common Garden Spider looks like a wasp to fool its enemies who would rather avoid wasps and also to fool the wasps it eats.

Spider defenses

Spiders have smart ways to defend themselves from enemies that would like to eat them.

1. **Break a leg** – If a predator, like a bird, grabs a Spider's leg, the Spider can break it off close to their body. Young Spiders can grow another leg. It will grow in curled next to their body and will appear after their next molt. Adult Spiders can't do this.

2. **Outa sight** – Some Spiders make a silk trapeze line, drop down it to the ground and play dead to confuse their attackers.

3. **Camo Spiders** – Some Spiders know how to simply disappear into the background, making themselves look like part of a tree or a stone. Some Orb Spiders use this strategy, making themselves look like a twig or leaf bud during the day when their enemies are active.

4. **Fooler Spiders** – These Spiders fool birds by pretending they're bird poop. This Spider defense works really well for Dung Spiders and Bird Dropping Spiders.

5. **Mimicry Spiders** – Mimicry means acting like another, more dangerous bug to scare off an enemy. *Amyciaea albomaculata* is a Spider that can mimic, or make itself smell exactly like a Green Tree Ant. This fools birds into thinking this Spider actually is a Green Tree Ant, which the birds steer clear of because Green Tree Ants are fierce stingers and biters. The Spider gets a double win, scaring off the birds and then eating the ants who are also fooled into thinking the Spider smells friendly enough to be one of their gang.

Experiments in 2020 proved that Spiders have difficulty building their webs in zero gravity. However, when they are in zero gravity but there is a light on, the Spiders get their directions from where the light is coming from as if it was the sun. Using the sun as their guide to what is above them, they can build their normal webs in zero gravity!

A Huntsman Spider mother with Spiderlings.

Spider babies

It's dangerous to be a male Spider in love. That's because, unlike almost every other animal, female Spiders are practical. They think that after mating the males would make a good snack. Male Spiders have different strategies to avoid this. Some rush away right after mating. Others hope that their intricate courtship dances will keep them alive. Sometimes this works.

Females lay as many as 3,000 eggs. Most female Spiders make a platform of silk for their eggs, lay several hundred, then wrap the eggs in silk to protect them from predators, parasites, bad weather or rain. Then they lay more eggs and repeat.

Most Spiders aren't very good parents. Females of some types of Spiders carry their egg cocoons around with them, protecting them for 2 to 3 weeks until the babies hatch. Or Spider mothers might attach the cocoon to the underside of a leaf and stay to guard it, not even leaving to hunt. If any insects get caught in her cocoons, the mother Spider will eat them.

Spider babies are called Spiderlings.

How do Spiders get around?

Spiders can't fly, but some of them can rappel using their silk. All of them can walk and some can walk or run on water.

Some have these and even stranger ways to get around. Ballooning Spiders can stand up straight, raise the underside of their abdomen up to the sky, make some strands of silk and take off, floating on air currents for long distances. Sometimes this can be for many miles or kilometers, even on days that aren't breezy.

Spider silk picks up a negative electric charge as it leaves their body so the Spider is repelled by negative-charged plants. That force is enough to launch them into the air. After that, these Spiders travel for free on breezes and air currents.

Electrical fields on plants are the strongest at the edges of the plants, and Ballooning Spiders know this. They know they'll get a successful launch if they balloon from twigs or the tips of blades of grass. Then they are carried along partly by negative electric charges in the air.

All Spiders can run and walk, and some of them can glide!

Ballooning Spiders take their flying journeys to avoid too much competition for food or their enemies or to find food. Ballooning Spiders have been found 1,000 miles or 1,609 kilometers out to sea and up to 2.5 miles or 4 kilometers up in the air. That's almost as high as a long-distance plane flies.

Ballooning Spiders can't choose where they go or change direction. They have to go where the electrical charges and air currents take them.

Spider webs

Most Spiders don't make webs. Only about 1/3 (or one out of every three species) do. In their millions of years on earth, Spiders who are web-spinners have evolved a huge variety of designs for their own bodies and for their webs.

A Spider's web is a trap to catch prey. Some scientists also believe that a Spider's web is like a part of their brain. Spiders, they say, think with their brains but also with their webs that are tuned in to their brains.

If you put a Spider that just had a big meal onto the web of a very hungry Spider and these two Spiders don't meet up and try to eat each other, the not-hungry Spider will still eat any flies it finds stored on the web. It's as if the web told it to still be hungry, even when it isn't. So, the scientists say, is the web helping the Spider think? What do *you* think about that?

A Spider can change its own body to adjust its vibration sensors on its joints to different vibrational

Some web Spiders replace their webs every day. Others simply fix the damage, sometimes several times a day.

frequencies just by changing how it is standing on its web. Vibration means something moving back and forth, over and over. How fast it is moving is the vibration frequency. Web Spiders can know not just that their web is moving, but how fast it's moving and where it's moving. This helps tell Spiders what is moving on their web before they rush over to investigate.

A Spider can change the speed and strength of vibrations on their own web by changing how stiff their silk is, how tight the web strands are or the shape of their web. They can add tension (that means tightness) to the web strands or make the strands thicker. This is something like a musician tuning their guitar or violin. When you make the strings tighter, you change the vibration and the sound.

Web Spiders can also make some silk strands on their webs sticky. They place the sticky parts of their webs where they will catch the kinds of bugs they want to eat. Webs that are flat and horizontal (like a small ceiling above the ground) catch insects that fly up from the ground. Webs that are vertical, like a small wall above the ground, trap insects that are flying past and don't notice the web until it's too late.

Spider silk shrinks when it is humid or wet out. Rain usually destroys a web. Webs also get torn and messy or wear out quickly. Many species of web Spiders have to rebuild their webs often, sometimes several times a day.

Spiders place a tiny water droplet at each juncture or joining place of the web. The Spider puts a few extra loops of silk in the water so the web can stretch if it needs to without breaking.

Orb-spinning Spiders

Orb-spinning Spiders use their webs as traps for their prey, but also as surveillance or look-out systems, always on high alert for their enemies. These Spiders sit at the centers of their orb webs and rest their legs on the radial spokes of the webs. These spokes send vibrations towards the center when a bug is caught in the web and it struggles to escape.

An orb web is flat and round, like a plate.

The Spider senses these vibrations. Its web tells it where the vibrations come from and also how large the insect is that is causing the vibrations.

Orb Spiders live everywhere in the world except Antarctica. They are small Spiders, weaving small webs. Some decorate their webs with leftover pieces of insects they've already eaten. Scientists don't know why they do this.

At least once a day, many orb Spiders take down their webs for a total replacement. They usually eat their old web so they don't lose the protein.

An orb web is really two webs. The first one is a circle. The second one, on top of the first, is a sticky circle to catch anything flying past or that blunders into the web. An average orb web has about 60 meters or 66

A triangle Spider web.

yards of silk, with 700 attachments. There are attachments everywhere two silk strands meet. An orb in a good spot can catch as many as 250 insects in a day.

A Golden Orb Spider can make a line of silk up to 700 meters or 765 yards long. That would be the same as an adult man being able to make a thread that is 14 kilometers or almost 9 miles long, if humans had spinnerets.

Triangle webs

Triangle webs are just like flat orb or round webs except they have a triangle shape, like a sailboat's sail.

This is a funnel web.

Irregular webs

Irregular webs, also known as cobwebs, look like messy or careless Spiders made them. These webs are messy on purpose to confuse insects, birds or other prey.

Usually irregular webs take several days to build and last longer than simple orb webs. They also have only a few places that are sticky or none at all.

Funnel webs

Funnel webs are made by Funnel Web Spiders. All of them live in Australia. Funnel webs look like the round doorway to a cave tunnel. The tunnel is made of Spider silk.

Bolas Spiders

A bola is a throwing weapon with a heavy object, like a rock, at the end of a rope. A skilled bola thrower can injure or kill prey, such as birds, with a bola.

It could be that our ancient human ancestors got the idea for bola hunting from female Bolas Spiders. These Spiders perfected the technique of creating a line of their own silk with a sticky and wet glob at the end. They use it to attack and capture the male moths they eat. Only the females do this.

Bolas Spiders can adjust their bolas according to what type of moth they are hunting. To get close enough to attack, they attract the male moths using pheromones (say this: FAIR-oh-moans). Pheromones are smell signals many animals use to attract mates. Male moths use their pheromones when they are looking for a female.

Bolas Spiders know how to fake the female moth pheromones, attracting male moths to investigate – and be attacked. Bolas Spiders hit their prey targets half of the times they throw their bolas. If they haven't struck and wrapped a moth in their bola after about 30 minutes, they eat the bola and rest for a while, then make a new one and continue hunting.

Young female Bolas Spiders and all male Bolas Spiders do not make bolas. Instead, they can make different pheromones that attract moth flies. They catch these flies with their front legs.

During the day, Bolas Spiders disguise themselves as bird poop. They wake up and hunt at night. The

A Trapdoor Spider is a bit like a jack-in-the-box, only when the door opens, it isn't a clown that jumps out, it's a hungry Spider.

female adults can adjust their bolas depending on what type and size of moth they are trying to capture. These Spiders are very skilled at casting their bolas. They can catch a male moth that is flying.

Unusually for Spiders, the female Bolas Spiders are more colorful than the males. Bolas Spiders live in North America, Australia, and Southern Africa.

Trapdoor Spiders

A Trapdoor Spider will wait until it senses vibrations telling it that there is an insect walking near its own front door. When that insect gets close, the Trapdoor

Spider throws the door open, lunges for the insect and drags it into its lair, and the door shuts behind it. For the insect there is no escape. This can all happen in less than a second.

Trapdoor Spiders spend almost all their lives inside their burrows, waiting to grab a tasty insect. This is the most primitive type of Spider, very much like the earliest ancient Spider ancestors of millions of years ago. These Spiders usually live for more than five years and can live for as long as 20 years. Only the males ever leave their burrows, and that is only to seek out a female to mate with.

Their burrows are silk-lined tubes. The door has hinges and the outside of the door is disguised, nearly impossible for insects to see. Trapdoor Spiders also lay trip lines around their doors, helping to alert them of any passing prey.

Trapdoor Spiders can bite. Their bite is painful for humans or other mammals.

Spider Thieves

The Dew Drop Spider is a thief, stealing from larger spiders by hacking their webs. Here's how they do it. The Dew Drop Spider will run lines of silk from its own hiding place to the hub and spokes of another Spider's web. This is done to confuse the bigger Spider and to connect to that Spider's web. This way, it knows when the bigger Spider catches an insect and when it wraps that insect to eat later.

Some Spiders are thieves!

When the larger Spider leaves its future dinner, the Dew Drop Spider rushes over to steal the meal. Dew Drop Spiders are so fast and clever with this trick that they almost never get caught by the bigger Spiders.

Some other types of Spiders are also thieves, grabbing a free meal when they can. And many Spiders are cannibals, eating other Spiders and sometimes their own parents or babies.

The world's smallest Spider is Patu digua. It lives in Columbia, South America and is .37 millimeter or just .015 inch long. That's too small for humans to see except under a microscope.

Spider bites

99.9 % of all the Spider species on earth are NOT dangerous to humans. That's the same as saying that out of every 1,000 species of Spiders, only one is likely to bite you AND for you to be seriously ill from that bite.

There are only 10 Spider species in the world that we know whose bite can kill a human. The four Spider species that live in North America and ARE dangerous are:

- Brown Recluse Spider
- Yellow Sac Spider
- Hobo Spider
- Black Widow Spider

Every species of Spider can bite. If you are ever bitten by a Spider and worried that it might be a dangerous one, you need to see the bite happening to know what kind of Spider bit you. If this happens, don't try to kill the Spider. Instead, you need to catch it and take it with you to get medical help. If that's not possible, you will need to be able to tell the doctor or first responder exactly what it looked like. This is so they will know what type of Spider it is so they know what kind of antivenom medicine you need.

Spider bites always cause pain and swelling and can cause fear, but they are rarely dangerous.

Tetragnatha extensa is a small Spider that can run across water faster than they can run on land. Their water running helps them catch mosquitos.

This is a Striped Lynx Spider.

Fishing Spiders

Fishing Spiders can walk on water. They can use their back legs to hold onto or anchor themselves on the edge of the shore, and their front legs to grab prey insects.

Striped Lynx Spider

The spiny-legged Striped Lynx Spider doesn't make a web. Instead, females use their silk to protect their eggs.

They live in North America and South America and help to control pest insects like mosquitos.

Females mate only once in their lives. The Spiderlings hatch and launch themselves on air currents or breezes, ballooning to a new home.

Spiders in North and Central America

The most common Spiders in North America are:

- Daddy Long Legs
- Yellow Garden Spider
- Jumping Spider
- Hobo Spider
- Brown Recluse Spider
- Black Widow Spider
- Wolf Spider

Brown Recluse Spider

Brown Recluse Spiders aren't always brown. They can be almost white, gray, beige, dark brown or brownish black. Some look a lot like Cellar Spiders.

They have 12 eyes and build irregular webs. They are cannibals, eating other Spiders when they can't find insects to eat. They can live for up to six months without food. They have short lives, usually only living for a year or two.

This is a Brown Recluse Spider.

This is a shy Spider, but they like to live in buildings and hide under furniture or in warm, moist places like bathrooms. Most of them live in Missouri, Kansas, Texas and Oklahoma. There are no Brown Recluse Spiders in the Rocky Mountains or west of the Rockies.

Triangle Spider

Triangle Spiders are house Spiders that live in North America, Argentina, South Africa, the Canary Islands and Asia.

They eat wasps, ants, pill bugs, ticks and other Spiders, including Brown Recluse Spiders. They also hunt and eat fire ants.

Common North American Spider

Get up early in summer and you may see this yellow and black garden Spider making a new web, something it does every morning at dawn. A harmless Spider, it uses its web to catch wasps. See it on pages 20 and 41.

Daddy Long Legs

There are three animals that share this name. Depending on where you live, a Daddy Long Legs could be a Harvestman, a Cellar Spider or a Crane Fly. The odd thing about Daddy Long Legs is that two of these animals that are often called "Daddy Long Legs Spiders" aren't Spiders at all!

Harvestman

A Harvestman looks like a Spider, with 8 long legs and a round brown body. But it's not a Spider. It's an insect.

A Harvestman has no fangs, no venom and can't bite humans. They have a bad reputation that they don't deserve because a lot of people think they're dangerous and are afraid of them. In fact, they're completely harmless to people.

The average home in North America has 30 Cellar Spiders living in it.

Cellar Spider

Cellar Spiders like to hide behind toilets, or under toilet seats, or in any dark, damp corner of your home. They have long legs and thin gray or brown bodies. They're not dangerous, but you might just want to check things out before you sit when you visit the bathroom!

An odd thing about Cellar Spiders is a mother will carry the hatchlings on her head.

Cellar Spiders need to molt 10 times to reach their adult size.

Crane Fly

There are more than 15,500 species of Crane Flies. They live almost everywhere in the world. They look slightly like Cellar Spiders, but more like large mosquitos. Some species eat nectar. Others have such short lives that the adults don't eat at all. Their eggs are black.

They can bite, but their venom is very weak and not dangerous to humans.

A Black Widow Spider bite can make you very sick but you will probably survive. There are only three known cases in the world of Black Widow bites that killed humans. The last time it happened was in 1983.

This is a Common Garden Spider.

Black & Yellow or Common Garden Spider or Zipper Spider

This Spider lives in most of United States including Hawaii, southern Canada, Central America and Mexico. Their large orb webs are up to 2 feet, or 60 centimeters, wide but are irregular and messy at the center, where the female waits for prey. They eat insects and small lizards.

Happy Face Spider

This Hawaiian native gets its name because of the happy face pattern on its back. It is an unusually colorful Spider with yellow, red and black patterns.

It hides under leaves during the day and hunts at night.

It is usual for Spider females to be colorful and males to simply be brown or black. That isn't true of Jumping Spiders. Males have vivid colors but females don't.

Jumping Spider

People like to call Jumping Spiders the teddy bears of the Spider world. That's because they're cute, with two big eyes like puppy dogs. Also like puppies, they are very active when they're awake.

Of all Spiders, they have the best vision. They can see things that are up to 28 centimeters, or 11 inches away. This is super-vision if you're a Spider! With their 8 eyes, they have almost wrap-around vision. The only things they can't see are directly behind their heads. Two of their eyes point forwards, others point to the sides or backwards. All these eyes take up half the space on their heads. Jumping Spiders can see as well as a dog or a pigeon.

The big eyes at the center of their faces see patterns and shapes and can see in color. Their other eyes can only see things that are moving.

Another strange thing about Jumping Spiders is the older they are, the better their eyesight gets! Jumping Spiders can see UV light, which almost all humans can't see. (There are some eye illnesses that cause people who have these illnesses to gain UV light sight, but this is very rare.)

Even more remarkable is their jumping abilities. They can jump up to 50 times the length of their own bodies! To make their middle and back legs strong enough to jump, they can pump blood into their legs.

Jumping Spiders can change their hunting technique depending on what the prey is, one reason arachnologists believe they are the most intelligent Spiders. They stalk their prey, unlike most other Spiders who wait for prey to wander by or stumble into their webs.

Jumping Spiders are one of the few types of Spiders whose behavior scientists have studied closely. These Spiders have shown that they are able to learn very quickly how to capture an insect species, even when they've never seen it before. They will stop and think, considering what is the best way to attack their prey.

Scientists also believe that Jumping Spiders dream when they sleep. We know that humans aren't the only sleeping dreamers. Dogs dream and when they do, their eyes move quickly, called rapid eye movement or REM. Humans also have periods of REM sleep every night, the times when we are dreaming. Dogs also twitch their legs when they dream. Spiders have REM and leg twitching when they sleep, which is why scientists who study them believe that these Spiders dream in their sleep.

Jumping Spiders need mammal blood to attract their mates. They don't get it by biting humans or animals. Instead, they get fresh mammal blood by capturing blood-filled female mosquitos.

Portia Spider

Portia Spiders are a type of Jumping Spider. Like their Jumping Spider cousins, they can solve problems and have really good eyesight. They know how to plan an attack, meaning they are usually successful, even when they attack larger Spiders.

They do it by dropping down to another Spider's web from above on their own line of silk. When they reach the web, they twang it so that the other Spider thinks there could be a prey insect stuck there. Or maybe it's just a twig or leaf. When the web owner rushes over to investigate, the Portia Spider attacks.

Not all insects are doomed when they get caught in a Spider's web. A ladybug (or ladybird) is strong enough to walk away. Her tough exoskeleton makes it hard for any Spider to bite her as she sprays him with a chemical Spiders hate.

Wolf Spiders live in North America and most other places around the world, including Australia.

Wolf Spiders

Wolf Spiders are a tunnel Spider who often make their homes in lawns. There they wait to sense the vibrations of a passing cricket, their favorite prey. They launch themselves out of their tunnels, sting the cricket and drag it back into their burrow.

When disturbed they do sting people, causing a very painful, very itchy wound.

Two-thirds of all known Spider species live in Africa.

California Turret Spider

This Spider is a distant cousin of Tarantulas and lives on the forest floor. There it builds small, silk-lined underground burrows. The outside of its burrow is hidden by mud, moss or leaves. It has very poor eyesight, so it relies on vibrations.

Hyllus gigantus

This Spider gets to be called Gigantus because it is the largest Jumping Spider in the world. It's 25 millimeters, or almost one inch long.

Like all Spiders, *Hyllus gigantus* doesn't have very strong legs. To be able to jump at all, it needs to force blood down into its legs to stiffen and strengthen them. Once it does, it can leap 8 times its own body length, or just about 8 inches or 200 millimeters. That would be the same as you jumping from one end of your school bus to the other in just one giant leap!

Tree Stump Orb Weaver

Many things are strange about the Tree Stump Orb Weaver. One is that it only lives in rotting tree stumps in North America, Europe and Asia.

It eats the insects you may not want in your garden, including beetles, flies and mosquitos.

This Spider is able to adjust its own metabolic rate, depending on how warm or cool it is outside.

This is a Spring-Backed Orb Weaver. Also called a Thorn Spider, it lives in the tropics worldwide.

Metabolic rate means how much energy a body is using and how much heat it is making. A faster metabolic rate uses up more energy. For all animals, including humans, energy comes from food.

Another unusual thing about Tree Stump Orb Weavers is that they can live in many different environments, from rainforests to places that don't get very much rain.

Their enemies are birds, lizards and other Spiders.

The Spider that lived the longest that we know of was a Trapdoor Spider female who lived for 43 years in Australia. She finally died not from old age, but from a wasp sting.

These are all different types of Crab Spiders.

Crab Spider

Crab Spiders can rappel from their silk lines. They sit and wait for a tasty-looking insect to wander by, like a butterfly. Then they rappel down to catch it, grabbing it with their front legs.

They live everywhere in the world except Greenland, Iceland, the Arctic and Antarctica.

Crab Spiders are also called Flower Spiders because that's where they often lurk, waiting to ambush their prey. Most are brown or gray, but some species of Crab Spiders are bright green, pink, yellow or white. They get their name because they're shaped like a crab, with front legs that are a lot longer than their back legs. They usually move sideways or they back up instead of walking straight ahead like most Spiders.

Bowl and Doily Spider

This very small spider is just 1/5 of an inch, or 5 millimeters wide. It lives in North and Central America. It has a unique web strategy. It makes two webs, one above the other. The top web is a horizontal sheet web, like a plate that is floating flat above the ground. That's the doily part of their web. Under it is the bowl-shaped second web.

When the web is complete, a Bowl and Doily Spider will hang below the bowl, waiting to see what gets caught in the two webs above.

Grass Spider

This Spider is small and harmless. It also has an unusual web that is part sheet web and part funnel web. It hides in the funnel section but catches its prey in the sheet section.

This Spider lives almost everywhere in North and South America.

Whip Spiders

This animal looks like a Spider. It acts like a Spider. But, unlike every other Spider, it only has 6 legs because it uses two of its former legs as antennae. Antennae are something no true Spider has.

So, is it a Spider? If not, what sort of creature is it? Scientists aren't sure.

We do know that it lives in trees and only in Costa Rica. Whip Spiders leave their trees to hunt during the day, but in the evening they return to the same tree, and the exact same spot on that same tree every night, using its antennae to find its home.

This is a very aggressive animal. When it stings people, it can draw blood. Despite this, it is one of the Spider species that some people keep as a pet, because it lives longer than most other Spiders, usually for 5 to 10 years.

Wrap-around Spider

Wrap-around Spiders don't get their name because they wrap their prey. Instead, they wrap themselves around twigs during the day. They are so good at almost disappearing into the twig that this keeps them safe while they sleep. At night, they wake up and spin their orb webs.

Dwarf Cobweb Spider

This tiny desert-loving Spider spins intricate webs. The females are almost twice as big as the males.

It has the ability to change its color to match whatever it is close to, like sand or scrub bushes. Dwarf Cobweb Spiders are active at night.

Two-tailed Spider

Two-tailed Spiders don't actually have any tails. What they do have is an odd ability to confuse and terrify the ants they attack. When an ant wanders too close to a Two-tailed Spider, the Spider starts running around and around the ant faster than the ant can move and spinning the ant's coffin with its silk. The ant is doomed.

Most Spiders have blood that has no color inside their bodies but turns blue in the air. Other animals that also have blue blood are pill bugs, some worms and slugs. Ocean animals that have blue blood are crabs, shrimp, octopus, crayfish, scallops, snails, barnacles, clams, squid and mussels.

Black Widow Spiders live in United States, Canada, Mexico, Europe and Asia.

Widow Spiders

Widow Spiders are the most dangerous Spiders that live in North America. They are large, shiny and black. Adult females can have red spots on their abdomens, sometimes in the shape of an hourglass or two triangles.

They aren't aggressive and would usually rather run and hide than waste their venom on an animal or human too large for them to eat.

There are also Widow Spiders that live in Australia, New Zealand, South Africa, South America and Europe.

Black Widow Spider

Females spin a messy horizontal web and hang upside down in it, with their legs stretched out, waiting to sense that something has gotten caught in the web.

A Black Widow is always hoping that something in her web will be a scorpion. Even though the scorpion is 5 times larger than the Black Widow, the scorpion gets stuck in the web. The Black Widow rushes over, careful not to get stung by the scorpion's tail before she can sting it. The sting stuns the scorpion, she wraps it tightly in her silk, and the scorpion is a future meal.

A Black Widow bite is painful, and can be deadly, especially to children, if the victim doesn't get the antivenom right away.

One reason this Spider is dangerous is it likes to live in houses. About 3,000 people in United States are bitten by Black Widows each year.

False Black Widow

This is a Spider with many names including False Katipo, False Button Spider, and Cupboard Spider. In Australia, they are called Brown House Spiders. They look like and are related to Widow Spiders, but their bite is less serious. Even so, it can cause intense pain.

Web-spinning Spiders are born already knowing how to make their webs.

Brazilian Wandering Spiders are 15 times more venomous than rattlesnakes.

Spiders in South America

Brazilian Wandering Spider or Wandering Banana Spider

This large spider can be more than 6 inches, or 152 millimeters long. Not only is it big, it's aggressive, with a venom that is more toxic than Black Widow Spiders. It lives in Central and South America and is a night hunter on jungle floors.

Brazilian Wandering Spiders are sometimes called Banana Spiders because some of them hitched rides on bananas shipped to Europe and ended up in grocery stores, badly frightening some unfortunate shoppers.

Bolivian Bleeding Spider

Only a few animals have the same bizarre defense strategy that this Spider has. When it is threatened by a predator, it will bleed from its mouth, scaring the predator into thinking it is an unhealthy food choice.

Dinopiss

Unlike most Spiders, Dinopiss has excellent eyesight that is 2,000 times more sensitive than any human's! Their eyesight is so good they can hunt in almost total darkness.

Strangely, this Spider goes blind every 24 hours and has to rebuild the retinas at the backs of its eyes every morning. It has venom that kills almost instantly.

Spiders in Britain and Europe

Swamp Spider

Swamp Spiders float on the surface of ponds, waiting to grab small fish. After stunning a minnow with its sting, it drags the fish ashore to eat it.

This is a male Lady Bird Spider.

Lady Bird Spider

This Spider lives in burrows almost everywhere in Europe. The females are all black, but the males have red bodies with black spots, making them look like ladybugs. They get their name because in Britain, ladybugs are called ladybirds.

European Purse Web Spider

This Spider lurks underground, with only its fangs showing through the leaves. Careless insects who don't notice that the fangs aren't twigs are grabbed and dragged to its underground tunnel.

Some species of Spiders have no eyes.

Diving Bell Spider

Diving Bell Spiders are the only known Spiders that can spend their entire lives underwater, even though they breathe air. They live in Europe and also parts of Asia.

They weave their underwater webs between the leaves and stems of underwater plants in lakes or ponds. Like all Spiders, they have to breathe oxygen so they must swim to the surface, where they catch air bubbles between the hairs on their middle legs. Then they dive, storing their air bubbles inside the one bigger air bubble on their webs. It looks like a diving bell, the air helmet human divers wear for deep dives, which gives this Spider their name.

When they're underwater, Diving Bell Spiders can stick their heads in their air bubbles to breathe or eat. They spend most of their lives with their heads in their air bubbles.

They don't use their webs to catch tadpoles and insects. They have to hunt underwater. And they have to return to the surface frequently to grab more air bubbles for their diving bells. In winter, they can hibernate inside their diving bells for up to four months.

Some Spiders prey on bees. Bees can see ultraviolet (UV) light. Spiders know this and can adjust how much UV light they are reflecting to fool the bees who might not notice the Spiders hidden in or on flowers.

Green-Fanged Tube Web Spider

This Spider lives in Europe. It has a dark, hairy body and two big green fangs that hang below its face. The fangs are luminous.

This Spider likes to live in cracks in buildings. There they weave their tube-shaped webs, with lines of their silk reaching out from their hidden webs. When a silk line quivers, this Spider leaps out to grab the victim and haul it back to its web. Females lay their eggs in their tube web. When Spiderlings grow big enough they eat their mother and then scatter.

Feather Legged Lace Weaver

If you visit garden centers in Europe, Asia or Africa you might see tiny spiders, just 1/5 inch or 5 millimeters long. Their favorite place to live is garden centers where there is a variety of plants and they are mostly undisturbed in their irregular, messy-looking webs. They make their webs look like abandoned webs to fool their predators into thinking they've already moved somewhere else.

They sit at the center of their webs and play dead to fool their prey.

The country that has the fewest Spiders in the world is Iceland. Even so, there are 91 species of spiders in Iceland, none of them dangerous to people.

Araneus or Cat-Faced Spider

Araneus Spider

There are 650 known species of Araneus Spiders, mostly living in Europe. When threatened, females bite, but males would rather run away or play dead. All the Araneus Spiders are orb-weavers and all have an almost round abdomen.

Long Jawed Orb Weaver

This social Spider lives in web cities! It builds webs that can wrap entire trees in only one night and can extend to be 333 yards or 300 meters wide!

Usually these huge webs appear overnight on beaches. You would have to live in or visit Israel or Greece to see this Spidery natural wonder, since Long-Jawed Orb Weavers only live in these two countries.

Yellow Sack Spider

This pale yellow Spider has a body that is almost see-through! It lives in Europe and also central Asia. A scary thing about it is that a bite from this Spider leaves a terrible, open wound that doesn't heal without medical help and possibly surgery.

Spiders in Australia

Australia is known as the country and continent that has more dangerous animals than anywhere else on earth, including more Spiders that could kill you. Most of Australia's most dangerous Spiders live on or near the East Coast and in Tasmania, so if you live there or travel there, you need to know how to recognize them and where to get the antivenom if you get stung. One thing that makes them so dangerous is that they'd rather bite than run away or play dead, like almost all other Spider species.

Most Spiders in Australia are harmless to humans.

Spiders can walk on their own silk and not get stuck on their own webs.

Gold Orb Weavers spend their entire lives on their webs.

Golden Silk Orb Weaver

This spider lives in Asia, Africa and also Australia. It makes strong, stretchy silk that is yellow and looks golden in sunlight. Golden Silk Orb Weaver silk is so strong, people of New Guinea have used it for centuries to make their fishing nets.

These Spiders are larger than most, 2 inches or 5 centimeters long as adults. It is the females who make the webs. The much smaller males live on the edges of female's webs, eating some of the food the female catches.

They can change the color of their webs, from pale yellow to bright yellow to gold, depending on where the web is built and how much sunshine shines on it. They want the sun to shine on their webs because golden webs glimmer in sunlight to attract bees and other insects Golden Silk Orb Weavers prefer.

Their webs can be very large, as much as 5 feet or more than 1.5 meters across. A Golden Orb Weaver doesn't take down its web, it just repairs any damage and then sits, head pointing to the ground, at the center of the web, waiting for some creature to get caught.

It is possible to weave Golden Orb Weaver silk into cloth, but it takes a lot of webs, and a lot of Spiders, just to be able to make one garment. This weaving method was first invented about 200 years ago in Madagascar, but it was soon abandoned. It was just too difficult and expensive to collect the thousands of wild Spider webs it takes to make only one piece of clothing.

There are lots of reasons that Spider silk clothes will never be popular. Spiders are small, they make small amounts of silk, keeping them in captivity is difficult, they are territorial, they can become cannibals when they live as captive Spiders and lab-grown artificial silk is not as strong as wild Spider silk.

In 1999, Sugar and Spice, two lab-produced goats, were genetically engineered into being Spider-goats. They looked like goats, but their milk was rich in spider silk proteins. This experiment was judged a failure and today, there are no Spider-goats alive in the world.

In 2019, the biotech company Spider and The North Face made the first spider silk clothes that the company said might make sense as a business. They made 50 jackets and held a lottery. Each of the 50 winners won the opportunity to pay US $1,400 each for a luxury Spider-silk jacket.

Spider silk cloth has also been tested for making bullet-proof vests, but there's a problem. This cloth is strong, but it is also so stretchy that a bullet would stretch the vest and enter the body of a person wearing it which would seriously injure them and possibly kill them. So while Spider silk is strong, and it can be beautiful, it can't stop bullets. You aren't likely to see any Spider silk clothing where you buy your clothes any time soon.

Mirror Spider

This tiny spider is just 1/11 inch or 3 millimeters long. It gets its name because its abdomen shimmers like a mirror when this Spider is out the sun. On some types of Mirror Spider, it looks like their back end is a green, yellow and red disco ball that flashes with light.

Other types of Mirror Spiders have silver patches on their backs that flash like strobe lights and the Spiders can control. Possibly these patches are to stun their prey, though arachnologists aren't sure what these patches, or reflecting abdomens, do to help this animal survive.

People who are extremely afraid of Spiders suffer from arachnophobia [say this: AR-ACK-no-pho-bee-ya).

Australian Robber Spider

This Spider gets its name because it has the ability to safely walk on other Spiders' webs. This allows it to steal their prey that is already captured.

Australian Ant-Slayer

This Spider is only half as big as its favorite prey, but it is such a skilled hunter that it is almost always successful in capturing banded sugar ants. During the day, Australian Ant-Slayers hide under the bark of eucalyptus trees. They come out of hiding at night, where they sit on the tree, waiting for an ant to wander by. When one does, this Spider leaps into action, hurling itself at the ant by doing a cartwheel. It does a Spiderman move, attaching a piece of Spider silk to the ant mid-air, then twirling around the ant, who can't escape. For the ant, it's all over in less than a second.

Northern Jeweled Spider

This orange, yellow and black Spider uses color to trick its prey. It mimics the colors of flowers that its prey insects like.

It lives only in Queensland, Australia.

Some Spiders can get a tan. They change color if they've been out in the sun.

This is a St. Andrews Cross Spider.

St. Andrews Cross Spider

This Spider has a silver, yellow, red and black body. It gets its name because it sits at the center of its web with its long legs folded in an X shape. From there, it can shake its web to confuse its prey.

It lives in Eastern Australia.

Spiders can be dangerous, but generally they'd rather run away than bite. They don't want to bite humans, or any animal that is too large for them to eat, because that would be wasting their venom. They only bite when they feel so threatened that they have no other choice.

Peacocks are the rock and roll Spider!

Peacock Spider

This Spider gets its name because the male does a fancy dance, waving its legs around. It shimmies and shakes its brightly colored hind end, which it can puff out like a peacock in red, blue, yellow, orange, and green. Males don't do this because they're dance crazy, or maybe trying out for a dance contest. They do it to impress females and also not get eaten.

Even so, after mating, a female might inject her venom into his brain and eat him anyways.

Peacocks are a jumping Spider. Each type of Peacock Spider has its own dance. They are active hunters and not only do they have colors, but they can also see them.

One type of Peacock Spider, the Black Spotted Peacock Spider, has brightly colored polka dots on its abdomen.

All wild Peacock Spiders live in Queensland, Australia and are harmless to humans.

Australian Wandering Spider

This Trapdoor Spider is related to the Brazilian Wandering Spider and is one of the deadliest Spiders in the world. It's large, can jump, and usually lives in dry places like scrubland, where it mostly eats insects. The largest Australian Wandering Spiders also eat small mammals.

Its bite can kill a human, though it can't sting through clothing.

Spider silk is stretchier than rubber and stronger, when strands are combined, than steel.

Funnel Web Spiders are aggressive! Unlike most Spiders, Funnel Webs would rather bite than run away. The males are more likely to bite than females.

This is a Sydney Funnel Web Spider.

Funnel Web Spiders

Funnel Webs are another group of Spiders that claim the Most Venomous Spiders In The World title. They live on the Eastern Coast of Australia and in Tasmania. Their fangs are milked to extract their venom. It is used to create the antivenom that could save your life, if you were bitten by a Funnel Web Spider.

This program has been so successful that there has not been a single death from a Funnel Web Spider sting in Australia since 1981!

The reason they are often called the World's most deadly Spider species is that a human who is bitten and doesn't immediately get antivenom will die in 15 minutes.

Like many Spiders, Funnel Web Spiders throw their front legs up in the air to signal that they're about to attack!

Redback Spider

The Redback Spider, also known as the Australian Black Widow, is all black with a red stripe on the top of its abdomen.

It eats insects, other Spiders and small lizards. This Spider particularly likes to live inside mailboxes or under toilet lids. This Spider is strong, able to catch and drag prey that are much bigger than they are.

Females build their webs at night with sticky strands, then wait above their webs for ants to get caught.

A Net-Casting Spider building a net.

Then they drop down to grab the ant and haul it up to where they are hiding to eat.

This is another stinging Spider that likes to hide under toilet seats or behind toilets, so if you live in Australia or you visit there, check before you sit.

If you're bitten, you'll need the antivenom. Its sting is very painful to humans and can be deadly in as little as 5 minutes.

Net-casting Spider

This Australian night-hunter has excellent night vision. It spins its ultrafine silk into nets held between the tips of 4 of its legs. Then it hangs upside down from

This is a Red-Headed Mouse Spider

two back legs on a branch or leaf, spreading its front legs to spread its net, and it waits.

When it catches something, it wraps, stings and feeds before making its next net.

Mouse Spider

Mouse Spiders live in their silk burrows in Australia and also in Chile, South America. They always live near water. Their sting is painful and can make people very ill, but it doesn't kill humans.

They are a type of Trapdoor Spider and spend their lives in their burrows.

Dancing White Lady Spiders live in the Namib Desert in Namibia, Africa.

Spiders in Asia and Africa

Dancing White Lady

Dancing White Ladies get their name by tapping their feet. But they must get the rhythm exactly right, because the wrong beats for their type of Dancing White Lady could mean they're attacked by another, very suspicious, Dancing White Lady.

They avoid the hot sun of daytime deep in their silk-lined burrows and only come out at night. They eat beetles, wasps, weevils, small reptiles and, when food is scarce, each other.

Females live for only about 6 months. Males live only 1 to 2 months.

Sand Spiders

There is no antivenom for Sand Spider bites. Fortunately, they very rarely sting humans. They are an ambush hunter, burying themselves in sand to wait for prey.

Assassin Spider

The Assassin Spider lives on Madagascar and in Australia. It is a small Spider with a strange, very long neck.

Darwin's Bark Spider

This Spider was only discovered in 2009. It lives in Madagascar and has a strange ability no other animal has.

A Darwin's Bark Spider female can throw one long strand of her silk on the breeze across a small stream. It flies over the water, attaching, if she is fortunate, to a tree on the other side.

The first line of silk is a bridge line. When it catches at the other side of the river, the Spider works across it, reinforcing the first strand. She builds an orb web that hangs below the reinforced anchor line to catch any insects like mayflies that are hovering just above the surface of the water.

Then she sits and waits. With luck, a passing Dragonfly will fly in and be caught.

This Spider has the strongest silk of any that scientists have studied. It is just 1 inch or 2.2 centimeters long, but it makes the widest webs built by just one Spider of any Spider species we know. This web can span a river that is 30 feet, or just over 9 meters wide.

No other Spider species can build their webs over water.

Ogre-Faced Spider or Net-Casting Spider

This Spider lives in the tropical parts of North America, South America, Australia and Africa. It has excellent night vision and only hunts at night.

Net-Casting Spiders spin what looks like a fishing net between their legs. Then they sit, with the net stretched open, waiting to catch something. When an insect gets close, the Spider releases the net and the insect is completely tangled inside it.

As the sun rises, its rays burn the Net-Casting Spiders' eyes. They become blind in sunlight. They have to hide in fallen leaves and wait until it gets dark again to grow back their eyesight, which they do every night!

Ant-mimic Spiders

Here's a type of Spider that would rather be an ant. Ant-mimic Spiders do a lot to try to look like ants. They have a different body shape than other Spiders, with the skinny waists and narrow abdomens of ants. They wave their front legs over their heads, pretending that these 2 legs are ant antennae. This makes them look like they have 6 legs, like an ant, instead of 8 legs, like every Spider.

And that's not all they do. To hide their extra eyes, they have color patches around two of their 8 eyes, hoping their 6 other eyes will look enough like an ant's 2 compound eyes! They cover their bodies with bristles that can reflect light, making them look like shiny ants.

In some of the Ant-mimic Spider species, the females, who are bigger, pretend to be one type of ant, while the males pretend to be another. They also try to act like ants, walking the same way, not jumping even though they can.

Here's why these Spiders work so hard to look like what they're not. By looking like ants, they might fool some of their enemies, like birds, lizards and other Spiders, into leaving them alone. It also helps these Spiders catch their own prey, the ants. There is one ant-mimicking Crab Spider that pretends to be a dying ant. It does this so worker ants will rush to help it, becoming the Spider's next victims.

When Spiders are running or walking, they always have at least 4 of their 8 legs on the ground.

The Goliath Bird Eater is the world's largest Spider. They can have a leg-span of up to 11 inches or 28 centimeters long!

Goliath Bird Eater

Despite their name, Goliath Bird Eater Spiders rarely eat birds. Instead, they hunt for insects, mice and other rodents, bats, lizards, toads and frogs. They are a type of Tarantula and live mostly in the rainforests in northern South America from Venezuela to Brazil.

They are night hunters and aren't dangerous to humans, although they have hairs on their abdomens that they release like darts into the air when they feel threatened. These hairs have stinging barbs at the ends that can cause an itchy rash for humans.

This is a Tarantula. They live almost everywhere in the world where it is warm.

This Spider has another defensive move. It makes a hissing sound by rubbing its legs together to warn off enemies.

Goliath Birdeaters don't spin webs. Instead, they use their silk to line their burrows.

In some places in South America, Goliath Bird Eaters roasted in banana leaves are considered a delicacy.

Tarantula

Tarantulas are divided into two types: the New World Tarantulas and the Old World Tarantulas. New World means North America and South America. Old World means Europe, Asia and Africa. Tarantulas live everywhere in the world where it is warm enough for them, including United States, Mexico and Southern Canada. The only place there is no Tarantulas is Antarctica. They prefer to live in scrubland, deserts and rain forests and most of them live in South America.

Tarantulas live long lives, compared to other Spiders. The males stay in their burrows for the first 5 to 10 years of their lives, eating insects, mice and snakes. Then they venture out to find a female to mate with, a dangerous nighttime adventure. Males go on their search for love in groups, hoping this helps protect them from their enemies, birds and the Tarantula Hawk Wasp. Males might go for several miles, or kilometers, looking for females.

They aren't easy to find because the females are deep in their own underground burrows. Males must search by listening for vibrations the females are making as they move around in their burrows, which can be 12 inches, or 30 centimeters underground. When a male finds a female who might be interested, he thumps his feet to announce his visit, something like knocking on her door. Some Tarantula species do a dance to charm the females who come up to their doors to investigate. Others do a drum beat with their legs, as the female watches. If she's impressed, she doesn't eat him. Or at least, not right away.

If she lets him get closer, he will gently stroke her. This stroking sends females into a love trance that lasts long enough to mate and for the male to make a quick escape, before she can come out of her love spell and eat him.

It is risky to handle a Tarantula. They do bite and a Tarantula bite can make a human seriously ill.

Males generally don't live very long after mating, but females can live for 30 years or more. All Tarantulas are nearly blind, but they can make out the difference between light and dark.

Females lay as many as 1,000 eggs, but they only do this once every three years. Hatchlings run away from their mother's burrow as soon as possible because otherwise she'll eat them.

Can Spiders be pets?

Spiders can be fascinating to watch, but they aren't a pet that will ever get to know you or even be able to recognize you. They're interesting to watch, they don't eat very much and they are fine living on their own, which is why some pet shops sell them and some people keep them as pets.

But Spiders, including Tarantulas, don't make good pets. One reason is that they shouldn't be handled by people. They can and do bite, and their bite is painful.

Some types of Tarantulas are now endangered species because so many have been captured and sold as pets. This is true for the Red-Knee Tarantula of Mexico. All Tarantulas sold as pets are either wild animals or bred from captured animals. To help protect Spiders, and be sure they will survive in the world, they should never be pets.

How do Spiders help people?

To make antivenom to treat Spider bites, scientists must have Spider venom. But there is more that they are discovering about how Spider venom can help people. One way is using it in other medicines. Another is using it in pesticides, the chemicals that kill pest species like mosquitos.

Spider silk is hypoallergenic. That means you can't be allergic to it. Bacteria can't grow on Spider silk. For these reasons, it is being used as a coating for implants – medical devices that are put inside the body to help it work. Spider silk is also useful to close wounds and for skin grafts.

Another use for Spider silk is as organic coating on foods we eat. Using Spider silk wrapping could one day reduce or replace the plastic wraps that contribute to pollution.

All of these uses for Spider silk are cutting-edge. Some are still in the research phases, not available yet to help people, but they will be, probably in your lifetime.

Are Spiders endangered?

Climate change is challenging every creature on earth, including Spiders. Some are getting bigger, like the Wolf Spiders that live near or in the Arctic. Others are becoming more aggressive as they compete for food and places to live. And there are some, like some species of Tarantula, that are targeted by animal poachers to be sold as pets.

Unlike some other animals, not a lot is known about how endangered they are. And there are some people who believe that losing the Spiders would be not a serious loss to the world, but they are wrong. Spiders, like every other creature, have their place in complex ecosystems. They are food for birds and also some other animals. Spiders help control pest species like mosquitos and flies. They inspire human innovation in developing medicines and in design and engineering.

We need the Spiders, just as they need us to make the world cleaner and safer for the world we share.

Crab Spider.

Thank you!

I hope you've enjoyed reading this book of strange and amazing facts about Spiders.

To find more books about the world's most fascinating and fantastic creatures, including some that make great pets, turn to the end of this book!

Best wishes,

Jacquelyn

More Fun Spider Facts

Most Spiders don't have webs. Instead, they are active hunters or ambush hunters.

Spider Lake is a town in Wisconsin, US.

It takes about 30 minutes for an orb-weaving Spider to create their web.

Some Spiders change their abdomen color depending on what they have just eaten. Other Spider species are able to change their own color to match where they are, making it harder for predators to find them. One Spider that does this is Cyrtophora cicatrosa. It can change its body from brown to white almost instantly!

A Wheel Spider can fold itself into a ball and roll downhill on sand to escape enemies faster than it can run.

Spiders have no teeth. All their food is liquid.

Fun Spider Facts for Kids

The Paradise Flycatcher bird steals Spider web silk to line its own nest.

Spitting Spiders can produce silk in their venom glands.

Australia has the most species of Spiders including some of the most toxic ones, but most Spiders in Australia, and everywhere else, are harmless to people.

All Spiders hate the color blue, especially light blue. Scientists think this is because that's the color of the sky and spiders always want to be hidden from their predators, not out in the open.

Music or any continuous noise annoys Spiders because it confuses them and they can't feel vibrations from their webs.

When there's plenty of food available, a Spider will just keep eating and its abdomen will get bigger. When there's no food around, its abdomen will shrink and it can go months without food.

About Jacquelyn

Jacquelyn Elnor Johnson started telling stories to entertain her younger sisters, discovering in the telling what it takes to engage your audience! By age 15, she was a correspondent for the local newspaper and had written her first book.

A life-long pet lover, she is the bestselling author of 20 books about caring for and enjoying pets and animals, including the books in this Fun Animal Facts for Kids series.

Find more fun books at:
www.CrimsonHillBooks.com

Photo Credits

Thank you to these photographers:

Loved all these great facts and photos? Discover MORE about your favourite pets and animals in these books:

- **Fun Leopard Gecko and Bearded Dragon Facts for Kids**

- **Fun Reptile Facts for Kids**

- **Fun Dog Facts for Kids**

- **Fun Cat Facts for Kids**

- **Fun Pony Facts for Kids**

- **Fun Horse Facts for Kids**

- **Fun Bird Facts for Kids**

- **Fun Backyard Bird Facts for Kids**

- **Fun Dinosaur Facts for Kids**

- **Fun T-Rex Facts for Kids**

- **Fun Snake Facts for Kids**

- **Fun Bug Facts for Kids**

- **Fun Spider Facts for Kids**

Find ALL the books in this series at
www.CrimsonHillBooks.com